Biblical Zionism Series – Part 3

THE GREAT COVENANTS *of* THE BIBLE

Malcolm Hedding

INTERNATIONAL CHRISTIAN
EMBASSY JERUSALEM

The Great Covenants of the Bible /
Malcolm Hedding

Copyright 2010 by:

International Christian Embassy Jerusalem Hong Kong
Phone : (852) 6748 0533 Fax: (852) 2559 0062
Website : www.icejhk.org
email: colinandnancy@yahoo.ca
       icejhk@gmail.com

Copyright approved by ICEJ USA Inc to re-print in English Distribution only in Hong Kong, China and S.E. Asia

---

The International Christian Embassy Jerusalem was founded in 1980 as an act of comfort and solidarity with Israel and the Jewish people in their claim to Jerusalem.

From our headquarters in Jerusalem and through our branches and representatives in over 80 nations, we seek to challenge the church to take up its scriptural responsibilities towards the Jewish people, to remind Israel of the wonderful promises made to her in the Bible, and to be a source of practical assistance to all the people of the land of Israel.

All scriptures are taken from The New King James Version. 1996, c1982. Thomas Nelson: Nashville

All rights reserved. No part of this book may be used or reproduced in any form without written permission from the author, except in the case of brief quotations in reviews or critical articles.

CONTENTS

Introduction	5
The Abrahamic Covenant	9
The Mosaic Covenant	13
The New Covenant	19
The Fallacy of Replacement Theology	25
The Davidic Covenant	29

Introduction

There are four great covenants of Israel and each one of these covenants plays a vital part in redemptive history. These covenants are the Abrahamic covenant, the Mosaic covenant, the new covenant, and the Davidic covenant.

For many Christians these covenants are disconnected and they do not seem to fit together. But if we examine the pages of scripture more carefully, we will discover that all of these covenants are interrelated and connected, and together they fulfill the purpose of God for world redemption.

A covenant from a biblical perspective is a one-sided agreement backed up by the character of God. That is, the God of the Bible and of history sets the terms and conditions of a covenant and invites humankind to embrace them and by so doing, enjoy the benefits. The covenants are always redemptive.

According to the Apostle Paul, the nation of Israel mediates or gives these covenants to the world. Thus, Israel is God's birthing vehicle, and Paul lists the redemptive products she birthed in Romans 9.

> [1] I tell the truth in Christ, I am not lying, my conscience also bearing me witness in the Holy Spirit, [2] that I have great sorrow and

continual grief in my heart. [3] For I could wish that I myself were accursed from Christ for my brethren, my countrymen according to the flesh, [4] who are Israelites, to whom *pertain* the adoption, the glory, the covenants, the giving of the law, the service *of God,* and the promises; [5] of whom *are* the fathers and from whom, according to the flesh, Christ *came,* who is over all, *the* eternally blessed God. Amen. *(Romans 9:1-5)*

Notice that the apostle does not refer to a covenant in the singular but he refers to the fact that from the nation of Israel we have received the covenants (plural). Then we go to Revelation 1.

[4] John, to the seven churches which are in Asia: Grace to you and peace from Him who is and who was and who is to come, and from the seven Spirits who are before His throne, [5] and from Jesus Christ, the faithful witness, the firstborn from the dead, and the ruler over the kings of the earth. To Him who loved us and washed us from our sins in His own blood, [6] and has made us kings and priests to His God and Father, to Him *be* glory and dominion forever and ever. Amen.
(Revelation 1:4-6)

It should be noted that our destiny is not just to be saints or God's children. We are in fact called to be a kingdom. That is, we are kings and we will one day reign with Jesus over the world.

Here in these verses in Revelation we note that we are destined to become a kingdom of priests or kings

The Great Covenants of the Bible

by virtue of our being in Christ. Quite obviously we are already part of the kingdom of God and, to some degree, we do reign in life by Jesus Christ. However, there will be a fuller expression of this after Jesus returns as King of Kings and sets up His messianic kingdom.

This kingdom is inaugurated because of the implementation of the final great covenant of history, the Davidic covenant. In short, Jesus returns in the near future as the Root and Offspring of David. God's covenant promise to David will not fail! His great-great-great-grandson will reign in Jerusalem over the earth.

There are four great covenants of the Bible. They fulfill the purpose of God for world redemption. In fact, each one of these covenants plays a vital part in your life. Let us then examine more closely the four great covenants of the Bible.

The Abrahamic Covenant

If I asked a Christian congregation what is the most important covenant in the Bible, I am almost sure the response would be, the new covenant. And of course, that would be wrong! Now, I am an Assemblies of God minister. I would never lead you astray! Thus, I have to tell you, if you said the most important covenant in the Bible was the new covenant, you would in fact be wrong.

The most important covenant in the Bible is the Abrahamic covenant. It is the greatest covenant of all history. The covenant is made and confirmed in Genesis chapters 12, 15 and 17.

> [1] Now the LORD had said to Abram:
> "Get out of your country,
> From your family
> And from your father's house,
> To a land that I will show you.
> [2] I will make you a great nation;
> I will bless you
> And make your name great;
> And you shall be a blessing.
> [3] I will bless those who bless you,
> And I will curse him who curses you;
> And in you all the families of the earth
> shall be blessed." *(Genesis 12:1-3)*

Verse 7:
⁷ Then the LORD appeared to Abram and said, "To your descendants I will give this land." And there he built an altar to the LORD, who had appeared to him.   *(Genesis 12:7)*

Why do we say this is the greatest of all of the covenants? Because the Abrahamic covenant is the covenant of decision. It constitutes God's decision to save the world. He says that through Abraham He will reach out to all the families of the earth – the whole world.

The new covenant is the covenant of ability. It constitutes God's ability to save the world. So the new covenant is perhaps the most essential covenant in the Bible, but the Abrahamic covenant is the most important covenant in the Bible.

Let me put it this way. If you need $200,000 by tomorrow morning and I have millions of dollars, the fact that I have the money does not help you. What you really need is a decision from me to give you the money.

And this is how we understand the difference between the Abrahamic covenant and the new covenant. Speaking reverently, the Lord Jesus is the $200,000 and the Abrahamic covenant is God's decision to give it. It is His decision to save the world.

That is why you will be interested to know that according to the New Testament scriptures, the first proclamation of the gospel was the Abrahamic covenant. The gospel did not begin with Matthew as

The Great Covenants of the Bible

many Christians think. The gospel began 4,000 years ago with Abraham.

> [8] And the Scripture, foreseeing that God would justify the Gentiles by faith, preached the gospel to Abraham beforehand, *saying, "In you all the nations shall be blessed."*
> *(Galatians 3:8)*

So the first proclamation of the gospel was given to Abraham when God told him that He had taken a decision to save the world, to find a lost world.

This is why it is always important to realize - and it might be a technical point for many - but it is true that no one ever found Jesus, because Jesus was not lost. Jesus found us because we were lost!

The Abrahamic covenant is the decision that God makes to save the world, so it is the greatest covenant of all history. It is also the covenant that establishes the nation of Israel and the land of Canaan as the vehicle of world redemption.

How can God communicate to the fallen world His decision to save it? He does it by the Abrahamic covenant that does two things. First, it constitutes His decision to save the world, and secondly, it brings into being the nation of Israel as the vehicle of world redemption. She will be the means by which this decision to save the world is made known to the world in time.

So the new covenant is the covenant of ability. It is the most essential covenant in the Bible with the Abrahamic covenant being the most important.

All the covenants are interconnected, as we shall learn in this booklet, because the Abrahamic covenant on its own cannot do what God has promised. He has to add to the Abrahamic covenant three other great covenants in order to accomplish His decision to save the world.

The Mosaic Covenant

The problem with our world is, if you go to a person on the street and you say to them, "You need to be saved," they will most likely look at you and say, "Are you kidding? From what?" The world is not generally convinced that it needs to be saved.

So God's decision to save the world, on its own, is not good enough. He has to add something to the Abrahamic covenant. And that is exactly what He did. He added the Mosaic covenant.

The Mosaic covenant refers to the giving of the law on Mount Sinai. Let us read in Exodus 19 what the Lord said to Moses about the law He was about to set forth.

> [3] And Moses went up to God, and the LORD called to him from the mountain, saying, "Thus you shall say to the house of Jacob, and tell the children of Israel: [4] 'You have seen what I did to the Egyptians, and *how* I bore you on eagles' wings and brought you to Myself. [5] Now therefore, if you will indeed obey My voice and keep My covenant, then you shall be a special treasure to Me above all people; for all the earth *is* Mine. [6] And you shall be to Me a kingdom of priests and a holy

nation.' These *are* the words which you shall speak to the children of Israel."
⁷ So Moses came and called for the elders of the people, and laid before them all these words which the LORD commanded him. ⁸ Then all the people answered together and said, "All that the LORD has spoken we will do." So Moses brought back the words of the people to the LORD. ⁹ And the LORD said to Moses, "Behold, I come to you in the thick cloud, that the people may hear when I speak with you, and believe you forever." So Moses told the words of the people to the LORD.
(Exodus 19:3-9)

The New Testament is very clear that the Mosaic covenant, or the law, was added to the Abrahamic covenant and that its purpose was to lead us to Christ.

¹⁹ What purpose then *does* the law *serve?* It was *added* because of transgressions, till the Seed should come to whom the promise was made; *and it was* appointed through angels by the hand of a mediator.   *(Galatians 3:19)*

²⁴ Therefore the law was our tutor *to bring us* to Christ, that we might be justified by faith.
(Galatians 3:24)

So the Abrahamic covenant is the covenant of decision. It is God's decision to save the world. The Mosaic covenant is the covenant of instruction and in the context of Galatians, God added it to the Abrahamic covenant.

The Great Covenants of the Bible

In Galatians 3 the apostle Paul is showing the interconnectedness between the Abrahamic covenant, the Mosaic covenant, and the new covenant. He begins by saying the Abrahamic covenant is the first proclamation of the gospel, but men and women are not convinced that they need to be saved; therefore, they need a teacher. So God added to the Abrahamic covenant the Mosaic covenant.

The law has become our tutor to bring us to Christ (Galatians 3:24). In the book of Romans, the Apostle Paul says in chapter 3, verse 20 that by the law we have knowledge of sin. So let me tell you, we would bring more people to Jesus if we would preach the law more.

Now when we talk about the law, we are not talking about the ritual law of sacrifice and temple ritual. We are talking about the moral law that is known as the majestic law or the Decalogue or the Ten Commandments. This is the law that Paul is talking about in Galatians 3. And this is the tutor or the teacher that brings us to Jesus.

Something very interesting to note here is why the Methodists were called Methodists. They were called Methodists because they had a method. It sounds funny, but it is absolutely true.

We have this idea that the Wesleys were big, strong preachers - tall, robust men with big lungs. But if you go to John Wesley's house in London, you can see his little slippers. It is hard to imagine that this is the man that God used to shake a world with a method!

The Great Covenants of the Bible

So what was his method? Well, he would set out on his pulpit, which happened to be his horse. He would ride into a village somewhere in England and he would go into the center of the town. There he would stand up on the saddle and he would begin to preach.

For seven days he would preach from the Ten Commandments. He would say, "You shall not commit adultery." "You shall not steal." "You shall not blaspheme." "You shall not covet your neighbor's goods or his wife." "You shall honor the Lord your God." "You shall have no graven images before Him." For seven days the man of God said nothing about Jesus.

As he preached, the power of God fell upon hundreds and thousands of men and women, because the Bible says, "When the Holy Spirit comes, He will convict the world of sin."

My dear friends, people do not accept Jesus because their marriages are in a mess. Neither do they accept Jesus because they have a bad bank balance and are in overdraft. Neither do they accept Jesus because of any other subjective problem.

We accept Jesus because we have rebelled against the character of God, and the Ten Commandments are a written description of the character of God. So when we preach them, under the power of the Spirit of God, the Holy Spirit takes conviction to the human heart, which is followed by repentance.

But thank God that when we do come to Jesus, He teaches us how to run our marriages and how to keep

The Great Covenants of the Bible

our bank accounts balanced, and He sorts out every other issue in our lives.

John Wesley, George Whitefield and Charles Wesley, the early Methodists, would spend seven days, sometimes a little less and sometimes a little more, preaching the Mosaic covenant. The law is our tutor to bring us to Jesus.

Then they would leave town and after a short time, they would ride back into the town. By that time, one of two things was happening. Either the whole town was seething under conviction of the Holy Spirit or they were seething with anger! There were occasions when John Wesley was run out of town by a posse because of his preaching.

Normally he would ride into the village center and would stand up again on his pulpit. Then he would begin to preach about the cross of Calvary where the sinner could go and find forgiveness, where the sinner could be delivered from the curse of the law and find eternal life, where the sinner could wash his or her sins away in the blood of Jesus and be reconciled to God.

So the Mosaic covenant is the covenant of instruction and that covenant paves the way, according to the Bible, for the sinner to go to Jesus. If you go back to Galatians 3, you will find that this is what Paul says:

[24] Therefore the law was our tutor *to bring us* to Christ, that we might be justified by faith.
(Galatians 3:24)

And then if we read from verse 10, he talks about the new covenant.

> [10] For as many as are of the works of the law are under the curse; for it is written, *"Cursed is everyone who does not continue in all things which are written in the book of the law, to do them."* [11] But that no one is justified by the law in the sight of God *is* evident, for *"the just shall live by faith."* [12] Yet the law is not of faith, but *"the man who does them shall live by them."*
> [13] Christ has redeemed us from the curse of the law, having become a curse for us (for it is written, *"Cursed* is *everyone who hangs on a tree").* *(Galatians 3:10-13)*

Why did Jesus come and die on the cross? Notice the next scripture, the very next verse in context. Jesus died on the cross in order to fulfill the promise of God in the Abrahamic covenant.

> [13] Christ has redeemed us from the curse of the law, having become a curse for us (for it is written, *"Cursed* is *everyone who hangs on a tree"),* [14] that the blessing of Abraham might come upon the Gentiles in Christ Jesus, that we might receive the promise of the Spirit through faith. *(Galatians 3:13-14)*

The promise of the Spirit of God is God's very life that is imparted to those who in Christ are reconciled to Him. It is the promise of new life and this, according to the Apostle Paul, is the blessing of the Abrahamic covenant.

The New Covenant

Jesus died on the cross so that the decision that God made in the Abrahamic covenant could be made real in our lives. This was provided through the new covenant that Jeremiah prophesied about.

> [31] "Behold, the days are coming, says the LORD, when I will make a new covenant with the house of Israel and with the house of Judah— [32] not according to the covenant that I made with their fathers in the day *that* I took them by the hand to lead them out of the land of Egypt, My covenant which they broke, though I was a husband to them, says the LORD. [33] But this *is* the covenant that I will make with the house of Israel after those days, says the LORD: I will put My law in their minds, and write it on their hearts; and I will be their God, and they shall be My people. [34] No more shall every man teach his neighbor, and every man his brother, saying, 'Know the LORD,' for they all shall know Me, from the least of them to the greatest of them, says the LORD. For I will forgive their iniquity, and their sin I will remember no more." *(Jeremiah 31:31-34)*

As we read in Galatians 3:13-14, Christ's death on the cross brought to us the blessing of the Abrahamic

The Great Covenants of the Bible

covenant. If we go to the end of the chapter, Paul confirms this again.

> ²⁹ And if you *are* Christ's, then you are Abraham's seed, and heirs according to the promise. *(Galatians 3:29)*

It is interesting that if you belong to Jesus, then you are Abraham's children according to the covenant. So let me ask you this question: In what covenant do we stand as God's children?

The answer is, the Abrahamic covenant. How did I get there? I got there by the Mosaic covenant, the covenant of instruction, and the new covenant, the covenant of ability.

If you are Christ's, if you belong to Jesus, then you are Abraham's child according to the promise. As we saw in Galatians 3:14, Jesus died on the cross so that the blessing of Abraham might come upon the Gentiles in Christ Jesus.

I am standing in the blessing of Abraham. I am part of that covenant. How did I get there? I got there by reason of the Mosaic covenant and the new covenant - the covenant of ability.

If you turn to the Gospel according to Luke, you will find that Luke here records the eulogy of Zacharias. This is very important, not only for us, but also for Israel. And in a moment we will see why.

> ⁶⁸ "Blessed *is* the Lord God of Israel, For He has visited and redeemed His people,

The Great Covenants of the Bible

⁶⁹ And has raised up a horn of salvation for us.
In the house of His servant David,
⁷⁰ As He spoke by the mouth of His holy prophets, Who *have been* since the world began,
⁷¹ That we should be saved from our enemies And from the hand of all who hate us,
⁷² To perform the mercy *promised* to our fathers And to remember His holy covenant,
⁷³ The oath which He swore to our father Abraham:
⁷⁴ To grant us that we, Being delivered from the hand of our enemies, Might serve Him without fear,
⁷⁵ In holiness and righteousness before Him all the days of our life."
⁷⁶ "And you, child, will be called the prophet of the Highest;
For you will go before the face of the Lord to prepare His ways,
⁷⁷ To give knowledge of salvation to His people
By the remission of their sins,
⁷⁸ Through the tender mercy of our God,
With which the Dayspring from on high has visited us;
⁷⁹ To give light to those who sit in darkness and the shadow of death,
To guide our feet into the way of peace."
(Luke 1:68-79)

Zacharias, under the power of the Spirit of God, prophesies the coming of John the Baptist, who is also the forerunner of the Messiah, and here we have this wonderful eulogy of praise to God for His faithfulness to His promises made centuries before.

John the Baptist and, of course, the Messiah have come so that God could fulfill His promise in the Abrahamic covenant. If you look at the passage carefully, you will discover that he affirms that John the Baptist, the forerunner of the Messiah, has come so that the promise that God gave to the world in the Abrahamic covenant - that He would save the world - can be fulfilled.

That is why the Bible teaches that the Abrahamic covenant has an executive arm in the Mosaic covenant and the new covenant. The Mosaic covenant and the new covenant enable what the Abrahamic covenant promises to become real.

The promise inherent in the Abrahamic covenant, that Israel would be delivered from fear and from her enemies, can only be made real via the Mosaic and new covenants.

The Mosaic covenant instructs us about our sin. Then to this covenant was added the covenant of ability where Jesus died on the cross for each one of us. His finished work alone is the means by which we are saved. These two covenants fulfill the promises made by God in the Abrahamic covenant. The same thing is seen in the book of Romans, chapter 15. Here again the interconnectedness of the covenants is seen.

[7] Therefore receive one another, just as Christ also received us, to the glory of God. [8] Now I say that Jesus Christ has become a servant to the circumcision for the truth of God, to confirm the promises *made* to the fathers,

> ⁹ and that the Gentiles might glorify God for *His* mercy....   *(Romans 15:7-9)*

In other words, Jesus came as a servant to the Jewish people to fulfill the promises that God made to the patriarchs, which is in fact the Abrahamic covenant. He came to be the executive arm of that promise. Therefore, He came as a servant to the Jewish people because the Bible affirms in Romans 9 that the covenants belong to Israel. We, by the mercy of God, have been allowed in. That is, the mercy of God extended to or through the covenants has brought us into the redemptive purpose of God.

So it is in Romans 15:27, we are reminded that all things pertaining to redemption are Jewish.

> ²⁷ It pleased them indeed, and they are their debtors. For if Gentiles have been partakers of their spiritual things, their duty is also to minister to them in material things.
> *(Romans 15:27)*

According to the third chapter of Galatians, the Mosaic covenant teaches me that I am a sinner. It is a covenant of instruction. My only hope is the new covenant by which my sins and guilt are removed by the blood of Jesus. This in turn means that I have been placed in the Abrahamic covenant, since it constitutes a declaration from God that He will be taking a very special family from all the nations of the world. All these covenants are mediated to us by the nation of Israel.

If you are Christ's, you are Abraham's child according to the covenant (Galatians 3:29). So I have a 4,000-year history. I am part of something that is wonderful! According to Paul, the first proclamation of the gospel was to Abraham 4,000 years ago (Galatians 3:8).

The Fallacy of Replacement Theology

Now, why is this so important? Because this puts an end to Replacement Theology. This is the final defense against the error of Replacement Theology.

Replacement Theology says that God has annulled His Abrahamic covenant. Therefore, there is no longer any destiny for Israel in the land of Canaan. That the church has now replaced Israel and she (that is, Israel) no longer enjoys a unique destiny in Zion. That is Replacement Theology.

That means in turn that there are many fellowships, mainly in the reformed tradition of the church, that see absolutely nothing in the restoration of the nation of Israel in our time. It is a political coincidence. It has nothing to do with the purposes of God, and Israel is just like any other nation. In short, there is nothing peculiar in the plan of God about her restoration.

This is the basic theory behind Replacement Theology. For this theory to hold water, it must rest on the notion that the Abrahamic covenant has been annulled, because it is the Abrahamic covenant that bequeaths to the people of Israel the land of Israel as an everlasting possession and their historical mission to bless the world.

Thus, if the Abrahamic covenant has been annulled, then how can I, a believer in Jesus, be Abraham's child according to that covenant? That is, if the covenant no longer exists, how can I be in it? Paul's affirmation just cannot be true. Moreover, how is it possible to receive the coming of the Spirit, the promised blessing of the Abrahamic covenant, if the promise has been removed?

If Replacement Theology is true, then what Paul is saying in the book of Galatians is not true. I am not Abraham's child according to the covenant. And the blessing of God that He promised in Abraham has not come upon me. After all, God has annulled the covenant! If He has annulled the covenant, then He must have also withdrawn His decision to save the world.

Paul says in the book of Galatians, as we have seen, that the gospel was first preached to Abraham in that covenant. So if God has withdrawn the Abrahamic covenant, He has withdrawn His decision to save the world. How many of you believe that? It is just not possible.

The Abrahamic covenant is not only the decision to save the world, it also is that covenant that brings into existence the vehicle of world redemption - the nation of Israel and her eternal right to the land of Canaan (Genesis 17:7-8). The conflict that rages today over this land is nothing short of the age-old one employed by the forces of darkness to frustrate the redemptive plan of God.

Therefore, the return of the Jewish people to the land of Canaan in our time is not a coincidence. It is

The Great Covenants of the Bible

in fact the fulfillment of God's word and God's promise to Abraham. It has nothing to do with prophecy. Prophecy is not the foundation; prophecy validates the foundation. It has everything to do with God keeping faith with His character.

So the book of Hebrews tells us that we know that God will be faithful to us because He will never break His covenant with Abraham. Notice Hebrews 6. Notice the link between the Abrahamic covenant and again, the new covenant.

> [13] For when God made a promise to Abraham, because He could swear by no one greater, He swore by Himself, [14] saying, *"Surely blessing I will bless you, and multiplying I will multiply you."* [15] And so, after he had patiently endured, he obtained the promise. [16] For men indeed swear by the greater, and an oath for confirmation *is* for them an end of all dispute. [17] Thus God, determining to show more abundantly to the heirs of promise the immutability of His counsel, confirmed *it* by an oath, [18] that by two immutable things, in which it *is* impossible for God to lie, we might have strong consolation, who have fled for refuge to lay hold of the hope set before *us.*
> [19] This *hope* we have as an anchor of the soul, both sure and steadfast, and which enters the Presence *behind* the veil, [20] where the forerunner has entered for us, *even* Jesus, having become High Priest forever according to the order of Melchizedek.
>
> *(Hebrews 6:13-20)*

The Great Covenants of the Bible

Fascinating passage! He says in essence that in the Abrahamic covenant, God promised salvation, that He will multiply and multiply thousands of people and bring them into the kingdom of God. Romans 4:13 says that when God spoke to Abraham, He promised him that he would be the heir not only of the Jewish people, but of the world.

The writer of the book of Hebrews says that God, wanting to show that He can never lie, swore by Himself and by His character that He would remain eternally faithful to the Abrahamic covenant. By this we will know that He cannot lie and will remain faithful to the new covenant. Jesus became the ultimate fulfillment of that promise. Therefore, we serve a God who is faithful, though those subscribing to Replacement Theology would deny this!

We serve a God who will never lie, but according to Replacement Theologians, He does lie. The whole of Replacement Theology, which removes a national destiny in the land of Canaan from Israel, is built on the fact that God has removed or annulled the Abrahamic covenant.

The writer of the book of Hebrews strongly refutes this. In his mind the promises given in the new covenant are made sure because of God's ongoing faithfulness to the Abrahamic covenant. He cannot and does not lie!

This is the real defense and only defense against Replacement Theology, because it demonstrates the weak foundations upon which Replacement Theology has been built.

The Davidic Covenant

In Psalm 105 the psalmist rejoices over the Abrahamic covenant. This is long after the Mosaic covenant has been given. In other words, the Abrahamic covenant did not fail, requiring God to change His mind and introduce the Mosaic covenant, and then because of its failure again, cause Him to introduce the new covenant. That is not the teaching of the Bible.

The Abrahamic covenant never failed. It is the covenant of decision as we have seen, and was followed by the covenant of instruction and then the covenant of ability. In Psalm 105 the Psalmist is rejoicing over God's eternal faithfulness. Notice that he rejoices over the blessing of God's eternal covenant with Abraham.

> [7] He *is* the LORD our God; His judgments *are* in all the earth.
> [8] He remembers His covenant forever, The word *which* He commanded, for a thousand generations,
> [9] *The covenant* which He made with Abraham.... *(Psalm 105:7-9)*

This God is a faithful God. He will remember His covenant forever - the covenant that He made for a thousand generations. If a generation is 40 years, we are talking about 40,000 years; if it is 70 years, it is 70,000. We have only lived 4,000 years since Abraham. So for Him, forever is just an incredible number of years.

> ⁹ *The covenant* which He made with Abraham,
> And His oath to Isaac,
> ¹⁰ And confirmed it to Jacob for a statute,
> To Israel *as* an everlasting covenant,
> ¹¹ Saying, "To you I will give the land of Canaan, As the allotment of your inheritance."
> *(Psalm 105:9-11)*

He is majoring on the land part or the "vehicle" part of the covenant and He is rejoicing over Israel's national destiny vouchsafed by the Abrahamic covenant.

In our time, since 1948, the nation of Israel has been reestablished. We ask ourselves, for what purpose? We have seen from the book of Romans, chapter 9, that the nation of Israel mediates all the covenants to the world.

There is thus still one last great covenant that has to be mediated to the world. That is the Davidic covenant, the covenant of triumph. Let us read where God promises David that his throne will be established forever.

> ¹¹ "And it shall be, when your days are fulfilled, when you must go *to be* with your fathers, that I will set up your seed after you, who will be of your sons; and I will establish his kingdom. ¹² He shall build Me a house, and I will establish his throne forever. ¹³ I will

The Great Covenants of the Bible

be his Father, and he shall be My son; and I will not take My mercy away from him, as I took *it* from *him* who was before you. [14] And I will establish him in My house and in My kingdom forever; and his throne shall be established forever." [15] According to all these words and according to all this vision, so Nathan spoke to David.
(1 Chronicles 17:11-15)

Here we have the Davidic covenant first spoken about in a prophetic form. There is going to be a king and He will reign forever. What a wonderful prophecy! If you turn to the book of Ezekiel, you will find that Ezekiel 37 also speaks about this coming king, this prince.

[24] "David My servant *shall be* king over them, and they shall all have one shepherd; they shall also walk in My judgments and observe My statutes, and do them. [25] Then they shall dwell in the land that I have given to Jacob My servant, where your fathers dwelt; and they shall dwell there, they, their children, and their children's children, forever; and My servant David *shall be* their prince forever. [26] Moreover I will make a covenant of peace with them, and it shall be an everlasting covenant with them; I will establish them and multiply them, and I will set My sanctuary in their midst forevermore. [27] My tabernacle also shall be with them; indeed I will be their God, and they shall be My people. [28] The nations also will know that I, the LORD, sanctify Israel, when My sanctuary is in their midst forevermore." *(Ezekiel 37:24-28)*

Interesting. Now notice the fascinating reference to Jacob: "Then they shall dwell in the land that I gave to Jacob." Now, did not God give it to Abraham and Isaac? Yes, He did. So why does He refer to Jacob? There is a reason.

The Bible teaches that He is the God of Abraham, Isaac and Jacob. Why the God of Abraham? Because He is the God of covenant or promise. Why the God of Isaac? Because He is the God of atonement, of the cross. Why is He the God of Jacob? Because He is the God of transformation and reconciliation.

Therefore, when He speaks of Israel dwelling in the land, He talks to her by using the patriarch of transformation. Now we know that Israel's right of domicile upon the land of Canaan is dependent upon her reconciled relationship with her God.

That is why here, the Bible clearly refers to the land and refers to Israel as Jacob. Jacob speaks of a transformed life.

It is fascinating how correct the Bible is in every little detail. It does not leave anything to chance. So it mentions David and his coming kingdom and Israel or Jacob living in the land under his rule and under his reign.

Israel has gone home in our time to mediate the last great covenant to the world. Isn't it exciting to live in such a time? It is amazing! We are not living in post-biblical times, but in fact in biblical times.

The drama of the ages is still playing itself out, and here we are caught in a sort of vortex of time. Suddenly we have seen something happen halfway through the last century that is preparing the world for the arrival of the Davidic covenant in its fullness. Israel has gone home to mediate the last great covenant to the world.

Jesus, the Offspring of David

In the book of Revelation, Jesus is always mentioned as the Root and the Offspring of David. This is because this book of Revelation deals with His triumph over all that is wicked and sinful.

It is a fascinating book. It is not a book about chaotic events that take place and suddenly God intervenes by the coming of Jesus, though this is what some people think. Actually the book of Revelation constitutes those events that have to take place on earth, under the sovereignty of God, to prepare the world for the unveiling of Jesus. There is nothing chaotic about the book of Revelation.

Now Revelation 22:16 says:

[16] "I, Jesus, have sent My angel to testify to you these things in the churches. I am the Root and the Offspring of David, the Bright and Morning Star."

It is interesting to note throughout the scriptures that Jesus refers to Himself as the Son of God or the Son of Man. Here in the book of Revelation, the book of triumph where all that is good triumphs over all that is evil, the Lord Jesus depicts Himself as the Root and the Offspring of David. He is coming to introduce the Davidic reign or covenant.

This will be the time when He will reign from Jerusalem, rule the nations with a rod of iron, and ensure that year after year the nations come up to Zion to celebrate the Feast of Tabernacles. Theologically we refer to this as the messianic age of Messiah, or millennium (Jeremiah 3:17; Revelation 2:27; Zechariah 14:16).

We have exciting things around the corner. Let me tell you something, there is nothing to be afraid of in this world, because our God has not lost control, and everything that is happening in every corner of the world today is under the total sovereignty of the God that we serve. He is bringing His eternal purpose to a conclusion (Revelation 17:17).

The Splendor of the Davidic Kingdom

In Isaiah 11 you will see something of the splendor of the messianic reign, that Davidic kingdom that is coming. It is an astonishing picture, and it is wonderful.

> [1] There shall come forth a Rod from the stem of Jesse,
> And a Branch shall grow out of his roots.
> [2] The Spirit of the LORD shall rest upon Him,
> The Spirit of wisdom and understanding,
> The Spirit of counsel and might,
> The Spirit of knowledge and of the fear of the LORD.
> [3] His delight *is* in the fear of the LORD,

And He shall not judge by the sight of His eyes,
Nor decide by the hearing of His ears;
⁴ But with righteousness He shall judge the poor,
And decide with equity for the meek of the earth;
He shall strike the earth with the rod of His mouth,
And with the breath of His lips He shall slay the wicked.
⁵ Righteousness shall be the belt of His loins,
And faithfulness the belt of His waist.
⁶ "The wolf also shall dwell with the lamb,
The leopard shall lie down with the young goat,
The calf and the young lion and the fatling together;
And a little child shall lead them.
⁷ The cow and the bear shall graze;
Their young ones shall lie down together;
And the lion shall eat straw like the ox.
⁸ The nursing child shall play by the cobra's hole,
And the weaned child shall put his hand in the viper's den.
⁹ They shall not hurt nor destroy in all My holy mountain,
For the earth shall be full of the knowledge of the LORD
As the waters cover the sea.
¹⁰ "And in that day there shall be a Root of Jesse,
Who shall stand as a banner to the people;
For the Gentiles shall seek Him,

And His resting place shall be glorious."
(Isaiah 11:1-10)

Hallelujah! That is a wonderful picture of the world to come! Then, if you turn to Isaiah 2, we have that exciting picture of a coming period in time when nations will no longer learn war but live in real peace because of the reign of David's Son.

¹ The word that Isaiah the son of Amoz saw concerning Judah and Jerusalem.
² Now it shall come to pass in the latter days
That the mountain of the LORD's house
Shall be established on the top of the mountains,
And shall be exalted above the hills;
And all nations shall flow to it.
³ Many people shall come and say,
"Come, and let us go up to the mountain of the LORD,
To the house of the God of Jacob;
He will teach us His ways,
And we shall walk in His paths."
For out of Zion shall go forth the law,
And the word of the LORD from Jerusalem.
⁴ He shall judge between the nations,
And rebuke many people;
They shall beat their swords into plowshares,
And their spears into pruning hooks;
Nation shall not lift up sword against nation,
Neither shall they learn war anymore.
(Isaiah 2:1-4)

This is a marvelous picture of the conditions that will prevail under the Davidic covenant and the type of world that will be unveiled at the time when the Messiah comes.

The truth is, the nation of Israel has gone home to mediate this great covenant of the reigning King to the world. We are now the witnesses of this journey upon which Israel has embarked. Moreover, the Bible teaches that it is Israel's physical restoration followed by Israel's spiritual recovery that will bring the King back to Jerusalem.

Inviting the King Back

There is a remarkable story in the Bible concerning David. It is a story that Jesus, I think, picked up on. Just before His passion, in the last week of His life, He stood on the Mount of Olives and He looked over the city and the Bible says that He wept. Then He spoke to the city and personified it. This is what He said:

> [37] "O Jerusalem, Jerusalem, the one who kills the prophets and stones those who are sent to her! How often I wanted to gather your children together, as a hen gathers her chicks under *her* wings, but you were not willing! [38] See! Your house is left to you desolate; [39] for I say to you, you shall see Me no more till you say, *'Blessed* is *He who comes in the name of the LORD!'" (Matthew 23:37-39)*

Now, I am sure that all of you who have made that wonderful pilgrimage to the Mount of Olives have stood there on the crest and gazed down on the Kidron Valley. Before you was the Temple Mount and Mount Moriah and you saw Ophel Hill, which was

David's city. You gazed upon Mount Zion and you have gazed upon the Upper City. What an incredible panorama that is!

Just feast your eyes and as you stand there, you look down toward the Kidron Valley. At the very foot of the valley you have the Garden of Gethsemane in which there are still five olive trees that are said to have been there at the time of Jesus. It is probably true, since an olive tree never dies. That is, it splits open sufficiently for one to climb into it or even hide in it. Some say that because of this it breaks its heart but it never dies.

Up the hill is a little church called *Dominus Flevet,* which means "the place where our Lord wept." This is not a church for corporate worship. It is a small church dedicated to private prayer, meditation and reflection.

If you walk into it, the front of the church is just one glorious window that looks out over the city of Jerusalem. Here it was that Jesus wept as He left the city and went out and bewailed the fact that they had rejected Him.

He then stated that they would not see Him again until the time would come that they would welcome Him back. That is exactly what Peter said in Acts 3:

> [19] "Repent therefore and be converted, that your sins may be blotted out, so that times of refreshing may come from the presence of the Lord, [20] and that He may send Jesus Christ, who was preached to you before, [21] whom heaven must receive until the times of

restoration of all things, which God has spoken by the mouth of all His holy prophets since the world began." *(Acts 3:19-21)*

In other words, Jesus will come back when Israel welcomes Him back. "You will not see me again until you say, 'Blessed is He who comes in the name of the Lord'" (Matthew 23:39).

So if that is true, then I believe Israel should occupy your prayers day and night. He will only return as the King of kings when she invites Him.

I cannot help but think that Jesus was in one sense playing out a real-life parable because He is the Son of David. It is fascinating to see in the book of 2 Samuel, chapter 19, that there came a time when David was rejected by his people and was actually chased out of the city. He also wept as he went. It is a very interesting story.

David left the city weeping and went through the Kidron Valley and up the Mount of Olives and out into the Judean wilderness. He had been rejected in favor of a usurper. Afterwards he wanted to return and so he returned the same way he left, from the east via the Mt of Olives.

It is a remarkable picture, since it is like the one that will be played out now very soon at the consummation of the age. The Messiah will not come back to His people until they invite Him. He waits, in the east, waiting to return via the Mount of Olives. David did the same thing.

¹¹ So King David sent to Zadok and Abiathar the priests, saying, "Speak to the elders of Judah, saying, 'Why are you the last to bring the king back to his house, since the words of all Israel have come to the king, to his *very* house? ¹² You *are* my brethren, you *are* my bone and my flesh. Why then are you the last to bring back the king?'" *(2 Samuel 19:11-12)*

The nation of Israel has gone home to the land of Canaan at a time when the gospel of Jesus Christ has reached the whole world - every tribe, every tongue, every nation - but the last to bring the King home is His own people.

He stands, as it were, before His people today. Just as He stood on the Mount of Olives 2,000 years ago and said, "You are not going to see Me until you say 'come home.'" With the establishment of the State of Israel, we have the emerging platform of His throne.

He stands again, as David did, across from the city and He waits and He says to His people, "Why are you the last to bring Me home?"

I am sure that when Jesus stood at *Dominus Flevet* He had this in His mind, because He is the Son of David. That is why the nation of Israel needs our prayers as never before, because this people has returned home to fulfill the last great task that God has given them, and that is to mediate the Davidic covenant to bring the King home, the Son of David.

The Morning Star Will Rise

There is a fascinating little story in the New Testament about the sign of the Davidic kingdom. The sign of the Abrahamic covenant as you saw from Psalm 105, is the land, something concrete. The sign of the Mosaic covenant is two tablets. The sign of the new covenant is the cross. So what is the sign of the Davidic covenant?

> [16] "I, Jesus, have sent My angel to testify to you these things in the churches. I am the Root and the Offspring of David, the Bright and Morning Star." *(Revelation 22:16)*

Then if you go to Revelation 2, you will find out something else.

> [26] "And he who overcomes, and keeps My works until the end, to him I will give power over the nations—
> [27] *'He shall rule them with a rod of iron;*
> They shall be dashed to pieces like the potter's vessels'*—*
> as I also have received from My Father;
> [28] and I will give him the morning star."
> *(Revelation 2:26-28)*

Notice the wording, for it gives us the destiny of the church. It is amazing! Jesus' privilege is to reign as the King over the nations, but if you remain faithful and if I remain faithful, we will be assumed into that same privilege. Jesus says if you remain faithful you will rule with Me on My throne and I will give you the bright and the morning star.

[21] "To him who overcomes I will grant to sit with Me on My throne, as I also overcame and sat down with My Father on His throne."
(Revelation 3:21)

[19] And so we have the prophetic word confirmed, which you do well to heed as a light that shines in a dark place, until the day dawns and the morning star rises in your hearts. *(2 Peter 1:19)*

So what is the sign of the Davidic covenant? It is the morning star. Why? Have you ever seen the morning star? You see it clearly in Israel. I have sometimes even wondered to myself, "What is that?" It hangs like a glimmering jewel against the backdrop of the approaching morning light.

The morning star is like a throne against a backdrop of light. The morning breaks, the night is gone, the darkness has vanished but there like a jewel in the light is the morning star. Like a glorious throne glittering in the heavens.

The Bible says that is the sign of the Davidic covenant. It reminds you perpetually that the throne of David, in a reign of glorious light, is coming. If you remain faithful that light will suddenly rise up in your heart, and before you know it you will be transformed and you will find yourself on the throne with Jesus. That, dear friends, is astonishing! Nevertheless, that is the promise of David in the book of Revelation and the second book of Peter.

[19] And so we have the prophetic word confirmed, which you do well to heed as a

light that shines in a dark place, until the day dawns and the morning star rises in your hearts. *(2 Peter 1:19)*

This is going to happen. David is going to come. So you must hold on to the promise of His coming - a coming that will be mediated by the nation of Israel. You must hold on to the promise of the Davidic covenant. You must be faithful in prayer until the day dawns, the breaking in of light, and the morning star rises in your hearts.

That is just incredible! Jesus says I am the Offspring of David. I am the morning star. I am the throne. I am coming. Tomorrow morning, as you get up early, as the light flashes across the sky and removes all the shadows of the night, look up and put your attention on that star. It shines gloriously, because it is going to rise in your heart.

Another picture of this is in Numbers 24. It is our friend Balaam who was asked time and time again to curse the people of God but he could not. Here he prophesies about the Messiah. Notice that the morning star is linked to ruling.

> [17] "I see Him, but not now;
> I behold Him, but not near;
> A Star shall come out of Jacob;
> A Scepter shall rise out of Israel,
> And batter the brow of Moab,
> And destroy all the sons of tumult."
> *(Numbers 24:17)*

What will bring the star back? Jacob. Why does He use the word Jacob? Transformation: it is Israel's transformation that brings Him back. A star will come out of Jacob and destroy the enemies of God. This star is the bright and morning star.

So, dear friends, the return of the Jewish people to the land of Israel brings us to the last great phase of human history. We have seen the mediation of the Abrahamic covenant. We have seen the mediation of the Mosaic covenant. We have been blessed and transformed by the new covenant. But I tell you, this redemption story will be fulfilled and brought to a conclusion by the Davidic covenant.

In your heart and in my heart will rise a star that will transport us to a throne, and we shall reign with Him over the nations. May God bring that day closer.

May we serve Him faithfully, and may we pray for Israel as she now languishes in the Middle East with the great final purpose of God hanging on her national destiny: to bring the King home.

Four-Part
Biblical Zionism Series

The Basis of Christian Support for Israel
The basis of Christian support for Israel is found in God's promises to Abraham. The Abrahamic covenant declared God's love for the world and his establishment of a people through which to redeem the world. Israel's unique calling is still in force today and her return home to the land given to Abraham is evidence of that.

The Heart of Biblical Zionism
Clear biblical principles concerning God's dealings with Israel and the nations are the framework for an accurate interpretation of God's promises and calling on national Israel. Biblical Zionism is clearly defined and put in the correct theological context in this teaching.

The Great Covenants of the Bible
This exciting study of the four great covenants of the Bible also refutes Replacement Theology which teaches that the church has replaced Israel and Israel no longer has a unique call or destiny.

The New Testament and Israel
The New Testament validates a number of Old Testament doctrines concerning Israel. Foremost it affirms that God has not gone back on His promises to Israel.

and Another
Foundational Teaching

The Celebration of the Feast of Tabernacles
The Feast of Tabernacles is a celebration of the triumph of the kingdom of God and as such is now celebrated annually by Christians around the world.

ICEJ
INTERNATIONAL CHRISTIAN EMBASSY JERUSALEM

In the summer of 1980, the Israeli Parliament declared the city of Jerusalem to be the undivided, eternal capital of the State of Israel, established as such by King David almost 3,000 years earlier. Protest resounded across the international political spectrum, resulting in the closure of all but three national embassies that were in Jerusalem.

A number of Christians living in Israel were then hosting a Christian celebration during the Jewish Feast of Tabernacles. They sensed Israel's deep hurt over the withdrawal of the foreign embassies and felt the call of the Lord to open a Christian Embassy in this, the City of the Great King. They called it the International Christian Embassy Jerusalem and it represents Christians from around the world, speaking words of comfort and support to Israel. Ever since, the Embassy has provided a "servant's heart" ministry to the people of the land. Following are some of our major programs.

ALIYAH

Enables Christians to assist in the immigration and absorption of Jews from around the world. Projects have included helping more than 100,000 Jews to leave the former Soviet Union by either plane or bus to return to Israel. Our teams travel throughout numerous countries assisting and encouraging potential Jewish emigrants in the tedious process of relocating to Israel.

IMMIGRANT SUPPORT

Assists newly arriving immigrants from around the world with dental and medical needs, distribution of food vouchers and clothes, and emergency housing. A home has been established for the initial care of arriving immigrants as they face the challenges of a new life in Israel.

SOCIAL ASSISTANCE PROGRAM
Works with local Israeli agencies to provide financial, practical, and spiritual support to needy people. Many joint projects have helped build bridges between different ethnic and religious communities, and have provided a witness to the providential love of God. Thousands of lives have been touched including Jews, Arabs, Christians, Muslims, Druze, Ethiopians, and Bedouins. Projects have included food, dental care, computer equipment, hearing aids, oxygen tanks, furniture, sheets, shoes, coats, an ambulance, a medical clinic, playground equipment, heaters, educational classes, and much more.

CHRISTIAN CELEBRATION DURING THE FEAST OF TABERNACLES
Brings thousands of Christians from over 100 nations to Jerusalem each year for a week of celebration, worship, and teaching during the only Jewish feast which instructs both Jew and Gentile to gather together before the Lord in Jerusalem to offer a sacrifice of thanksgiving.

INFORMATION MINISTRY
The ICEJ publishes a magazine "Word from Jerusalem" in different languages for worldwide distribution. Our website is a good source of information and the ICEJ's news service via the internet covers current issues affecting Israel's security and future. Quite often the Embassy's public affairs department issues statements and press releases on crucial matters. The Embassy also supplies thousands of audio and video teaching tapes explaining why Christians need to support God's purposes for Israel and Jerusalem.

INTERNATIONAL MINISTRY
The International Christian Embassy Jerusalem has representation in over 80 countries around the world. These branches regularly organize Israel Awareness events in their own countries, and plant seeds of love and support for Israel in local congregations. These include pro-Israel marches and petitions aimed toward governments and people of influence and they endeavor to challenge the nations from a biblical perspective concerning policies toward Israel.

Notes